Pocket Plays

13 ten-minute funny skits
for 6-18 year-old future thespians

by Dave Wood & Dave Ludlow

*No rehearsal, props or talent required - just a handful
of enthusiastic young people and a poor,
misguided leader to help maintain order!*

Cover and Illustrations: Ron Branagan

Welcome to **Pocket Plays**!

This is a collection of short but funny (though we say so ourselves!) plays that we've written for a range of audiences over the years. Many first appeared in Scouting Magazine and have been performed at Gang Shows throughout the country. Some scripts are old, some are new but all are guaranteed to give the performers and those in the audience a rib-tickling time!

They can be used in a variety of settings to very good effect...

- **Shows:** Great 'fillers' or 'front of tabs' items. Performers can wear suitable costumes and learn the lines or they can stand around microphones as on a radio show and simply wear a suitable hat for their character.

- **Teambuilding:** Hand out copies of a script, allocate parts to individuals and, with no practice, see how they perform!

- **Youth Groups:** Half an hour's practice will be enough for small groups of young people to rehearse a script and perform as a 'radio play'.

With each play, a key feature is the inclusion of a 'sound effects engineer'. This is often the most amusing part of the play, as someone tasked with the job tries with their voice or a gathered assortment of items to produce suitable effects at the appropriate time. For your convenience, we've given a few ideas of what could be included sound-wise alongside appropriate parts of each script.

But that's not all!

If you enjoy these scripts, there's another eight available by mail order! **POCKET PLAYS - THE DIRECTOR'S CUT!** is a disk holding all 13 plays contained in this book, PLUS a further EIGHT plays to complete your collection. For a copy of the disk contact Printforce at the address on the back of this book. A discount voucher appears on page 4 to thank you for buying both versions.

Anyway, even if you don't perform the plays in this book, we're sure you'll have a laugh reading them. Remember, if you enjoy reading them half as much as we do; we'll enjoy them twice as much as you!

Have fun!

Dave Wood & Dave Ludlow *February 2001*

CONTENTS

COMING SOON FROM THE SAME AUTHORS:

Very short mystery 'whodunnit'-style play entitled 'The Postman did it'

ACKNOWLEDGMENTS

Many thanks to The Editor(s) of Scouting Magazine for supporting this project over the years; to all the shows and comedians who inspired or 'lent' some of the gags; to our wives and children for putting up with our noisy writing sessions; and to Dave's mum's endless supply of Bakewell Tarts, under the influence of which many of these scripts were written. Special thanks go to the Acme Christmas Cracker Company (Penge) plc, without whom many of these scripts would not exist. Further thanks go to the following individuals, who have helped in the proof reading of this book and without whome many inacuracys would have krept in, so many thanks to

Pocket Plays – The Directors Cut

A disk holding all 13 plays contained in the book PLUS a further EIGHT plays.

Whilst the additional eight were published in Scouting Magazine between 1990 and 2000, all have been updated for 21st Century audiences! The disk (which is IBM PC and Apple Mac compatible) contains three different versions of the plays to enable you to print out larger copies for your cast members: **.pdf** file (use Adobe Acrobat Reader to read this); **.txt** files (plain text files which can be inserted into any word processing program) and **.htm** files (readable with an internet browser - but no internet access is required!).

This voucher is worth 50p against the purchase of the disk version of *Pocket Plays - The Director's Cut*, containing the 13 scripts in this book, plus a further 8 scripts.

50p

one voucher per transaction. voucher cannot be redeemed for cash. cash value 0.0001p
offer subject to availability. Printforce Ltd.

Gardeners' Questioning Time

THE CAST

Narrator – a narrator
Inspector Thinkalott – a clever detective
Whitsun – his bumbling assistant
Paddy Fields – a farmer
Feller – a baddie

Narrator:	'Twas the night before Christmas... and all through the police station in the tiny hamlet of Little Doing, nothing was stirring, save for the teaspoons in the teacups of Inspector Thinkalott and his bumbling assistant, Whitsun.	*Teaspoons stirring in mugs.*
Inspector:	Ah, this is the life, eh, Whitsun?	
Whitsun:	Are you sure sir?	
Inspector:	Yes, although we'd better get our skates on soon...	
Whitsun:	Why? Has the village pond frozen again?	
Inspector:	I mean we'd better get a move on if we're to decorate this police station before nightfall.	
Whitsun:	Why's that then guv?	
Inspector:	It's Christmas Eve.	*Christmas jingle bells/music in background.*
Whitsun:	I know it's Christmas, guv, but my name's Whitsun, not Eve. Anyway, I got that job lot of flashing festive lights from Cop Shop, the police equipment suppliers, because the garden centre had run out of fairy lights.	
Narrator:	The two detectives proceeded to festoon the outside of the police station, keen to make their mark on the sleepy community.	*Rustling of decorations.*
Inspector:	Here Whitsun, take this ladder. Be careful though, as it's not my real ladder... it's my stepladder. Righto, pass me the bulbs.	*Clunking of ladder.*
Whitsun:	Which do you want first guv – daffodils or tulips?	
Inspector:	Wrong box, you buffoon. Hand me those lightbulbs immediately.	*Box put on table.*
Narrator:	It was almost an hour later, when the two had used up the entire supply of lights that they stepped back to admire their work.	
Inspector:	Hmmm... perhaps next year we should get some colours other than blue. And possibly ones that don't rotate and flash quite so brightly.	
Whitsun:	Sorry guv – it's all they had.	

	Inspector:	Fair enough. However, the last thing to do now is to go and buy the Christmas Tree.
Locking door. Car doors closing and car driving off.	Narrator:	The detectives locked the station, got into their car and drove off towards the garden centre.
	Inspector:	The centre closes in 20 minutes Whitsun – you'd better put your foot down. I'll put the blue lights on as well to show we're in a hurry.
Revving engine.	Whitsun:	Ah, that doesn't work guv – the bulb's gone and the suppliers had run out...
Siren wailing, screeching tyres, cows, owls... sobbing engineer! Car stops.	Narrator:	With sirens wailing, tyres screeching, cows moo-ing, owls hooting and sound effects engineers sobbing breathlessly, they soon arrived at 'Sod-U-Love', purveyors of plants, compost, china models of frogs, cut-price cartoon videos, brass band CDs, chutney, framed pictures of someone else's children 50 years ago, teddy bears and other essential garden necessities.
	Whitsun:	We're going to be in trouble for arriving in a car guv.
	Inspector:	Why's that Whitsun?
	Whitsun:	On the sign by the gate it says 'Please drive in pot plants and pond liners'.
Walking on gravel. Dusting and gentle singing in background.	Narrator:	They entered the store and approached an assistant, who was busy dusting the pick-and-mix sweets.
	Guida:	Hallo my-a good friends. My-a name is-a Guida.
	Inspector:	Hello Aguida.
	Guida:	No no – not Aguida – just Guida.
	Inspector:	Right, *Jusguida*. We're after a tree.
	Guida:	No, its-a alright, there's nobody before you, I serve you now.
	Whitsun:	He means we want to buy a tree – do you have any?
	Guida:	Ah... there's-a none here.
	Inspector:	A nun? Alright, we'll speak to her then.
	Guida:	I mean we ain't-a got no real trees left.
	Whitsun:	Alright – we'll take a dozen imaginary ones instead then.
	Inspector:	Quiet Whitsun. Just tell me, Jusguida, what can you offer us instead, and I'm not interested in a double-glazed porcelain goat-shaped ashtray that plays 'Smoke gets in your Eyes'...
	Guida:	Oh – perhaps your friend would-a like it instead? Anyway – I can offer you this wonderful pseudo-real tree... Its needles they will not-a drop, guaranteed! It costs a little bit more but is-a worth the money and it's even got a built-in alarm to deter would-be thieves! £100 to you, I deliver tonight.

Narrator:	The two detectives gasped at the price.
W&I:	GASP!
Guida:	I'm-a sorry gentlemen – you think it's-a dear?
Inspector:	No, we're convinced it's a tree, albeit an expensive one.
Whitsun:	Yeah, guv, it's far too expensive – something's fishy.
Inspector:	That'll be the aquarium department, Whitsun. But I agree, let's return to the car and find a cheaper option.
Narrator:	They got in the car and drove off, determined to find a suitable tree. They headed for the largest tree farm in the county in order to get to the root of the problem. They were met in the farmyard by Paddy Fields, the farmer.
Paddy:	Hello gentlemen. Oi'll be with you in a moment – oi've just got to make sure young Jethro has rounded up the last of the saplings for milking.
Inspector:	We've no time for that, good sir. We need to purchase a real Christmas tree, and fast.
Paddy:	Why would you want to 'fast' after buying a Christmas tree? If it were me oi'd be tucking into turkey and sprouts!
Whitsun:	Come on – show us your firs.
Paddy:	Sorry, all the mink were set free by those animal liberation folk last week.
Inspector:	We want a tree!
Paddy:	Oh, Oi think they've all set free by the <u>tree</u> liberation front.
Inspector:	What do you mean?
Paddy:	Oi mean that moi entire crop of Christmas trees has been chopped down in their prime, meaning I haven't been able to supply any of the garden centres this year.
Whitsun:	You know what this means guv...
Inspector:	Yes Whitsun, it looks like at last this play has developed a storyline! Anyway my good man, you are in luck, for I am Inspector Thinkalott.
Paddy:	Thinkalott of the Yard?
Inspector:	Well, there's lots of cow dung on the concrete but overall it's okay I suppose.
Paddy:	Maybe you can help me round up moi missing trees. I caught a glimpse of the thieves – you'll be looking for tree fellers, begorrah.
Whitsun:	That's obvious, but I wonder just how many of them there were.

Car driving off and arriving/parking.

Walking across concrete.

Cow dung splats?

7

	Paddy:	There were <u>tree</u> fellers – oi saw them.
	Whitsun:	Well, if you find out how many there were, let us know.
	Inspector:	By the way – were any trees alarmed?
Rustling of branches.	Paddy:	Oi guess they were all a bit scared, in their own little way.
	Inspector:	I mean had you fitted any trees with burglar alarms?
	Paddy:	Only one – but that's been stolen too.
Walking through gravel, mud etc.	Narrator:	The two detectives made their way through the fields, following a trail of pine needles that led them to a log cabin at the farthest end of the farm. They approached the door with trepidation.
	Whitsun:	Go away, Trepidation, we're busy.
	Inspector:	After you, Whitsun.
	Whitsun:	Who is?
	Inspector:	I mean, you go in first.
Rattling of door.	Whitsun:	But the door's locked.
	Inspector:	Hmm... we'll have to go in the other way round.
	Whitsun:	How will going in backwards help us, guv?
Clanking of keys.	Inspector:	Oh forget it – just pick the lock then.
	Whitsun:	Righty-ho – I'll have this nice chunky black one.
	Inspector:	Doh! Just get on with it – I'll cover you.
	Whitsun:	But I won't be able to see anything if you do that, guv.
Door opens. *Grinding of machine.*	Narrator:	They eventually got through the door, only to find a room packed to the rafters with freshly-chopped fir trees. At one end of the room, next to a large machine, were three rough-looking men.
	Inspector:	You there – stop what you're doing! You're under arrest!
	Feller:	Blimey – it's like a small wooded patch of land... it's the copse!
Door opens, running feet/explosion.	Narrator:	Just then, the sultry Guida burst in the room. Whitsun mopped her up a bit and then arrested her too.
	Guida:	Hey, whatsamatter you? Gotta no respect?
	Inspector:	Hey – shadduppa-your face! Guida, you are under arrest for masterminding the stealing of 12,000 Christmas Trees, plus a large quantity of fairy lights.
	Guida:	What's the charge?
Sizzle of high voltage?	Whitsun:	About 240 volts.

Paddy: Oh, so you've caught the tree fellers! And one girl. Congratulations! But what's been going on here?

Inspector: It seems that these villains were using this sheep-shearing equipment to shave the needles off the stolen trees, which they then stuck back on to the branches with super glue.

Paddy: Why would they want to do that then?

Inspector: Simple – Guida had set up an internet dotcom company, comedyconifer.con.com, selling real trees with guaranteed non-drop needles.

Whitsun: So that's why there weren't any real trees in the shops – and people had no choice but to buy these vastly more expensive alternatives.

Guida: Mama Mia! You've-a got us-a bang-to-rights. But tell-a me one thing, Inspector. What put you on our trail?

Inspector: It was easy – Paddy here said that he had put a sophisticated alarm in one of the trees... and I recalled seeing such a tree in your garden centre – the one you were trying to sell us!

Whitsun: You don't mean...

Inspector: Yes, 'Alarm-in-tree', my dear Whitsun. Lock them up – I'll take one of these trees back to the station for, er, evidence.

Whitsun: And so's we can decorate it, eh guv?

Inspector: Yes, it certainly deserves a medal for what it's been through. Anyway, remember we've also got to find out who's stolen the knobs on the police radios.

Whitsun: Yes – we've not been able to turn anything up on that one. Then we've got to find out who keeps dumping vanloads of picnic baskets in the police station lobby.

Inspector: You're right – our investigations are being severely hampered.

The End

In The Drink

THE CAST
Narrator – a narrator
Inspector Thinkalott – a clever detective
Whitsun – his bumbling assistant
Sir Loinsteak – a rich toff
Roland Butter – one of his servants

Church bells, hooting of owl, howling of wind.	Narrator:	It was a dark and gloomy Christmas Eve in the lonely hamlet of Little Doing. Only the hooting of a distant owl could be heard through the howling wind. A car screeched to a halt in the driveway of Mysterious Manor and out stepped the somewhat daunting figure of Inspector Thinkalott from Scotland Yard. He slammed the car door shut and strolled up the gravel path to the front door where he met his assistant, Superintendent Whitsun, crouched behind a milk bottle. The Inspector spoke...
Car screeches to a halt.		
Footsteps. Car door slams.		
	Inspector:	Evening Super.
	Whitsun:	Hello wonderful!
	Inspector:	A brilliant camouflage Whitsun – that white coat and silver cap really had me fooled for a while. Anyway, why did you send for me?
	Whitsun:	Well guv, it seems that someone's killing off all the servants in Mysterious Manor in a mysterious manner.
	Inspector:	It's okay Whitsun, I heard you the first time. But tell me, have you got any leads?
Barking of dog.	Whitsun:	Only one sir, but there's this dog attached to it.
Doorbell rings.	Inspector:	Enough of this merry banter, ring the bell Whitsun.
Door opens.	Narrator:	The door opened and the owner of the Manor peered out and looked at the two men.
	Inspector:	Good evening, you must be Sir Loinsteak.
	Sir L:	That is correct, and you are ... ?
	Inspector:	Inspector Thinkalott – Thinkalott of the Yard.
	Sir L:	Well, I've never actually been there but they say the lunches are quite good.
	Inspector:	Sir Loinsteak, we've come about some murders.
	Sir L:	Not today thanks, we've already had some this morning.
	Whitsun:	Precisely sir, we're here to solve them.
Footsteps.	Sir L:	Walk this way then gentlemen and I'll show you the bodies.

Narrator:	Carefully avoiding a 'walk this way' gag, the two police officers followed Sir Loinsteak into the servants' quarters	*Footsteps.*
Whitsun:	What a dirty old room sir, are you sure they weren't just nibbled to death by those mice down there?	
Inspector:	Wait a minute, those mice – what have they got in their mouths Whitsun?	*Squeaking of mice.*
Whitsun:	Probably a tiny red tongue and a couple of rows of teeth Inspector.	
Inspector:	No Whitsun, I mean those pieces of lemon rind.	*Mice chewing.*
Sir L:	Gad, that can only mean one thing gentlemen.	
Whitsun:	You mean that mice like lemons?	
Sir L:	Yes, but those lemons could only have come from one place! Follow me to the wine cellar!	*Footsteps.*
Whitsun:	But I don't want to buy any wine.	
Narrator:	They arrived in the cellar, where Roland Butter was busy bottling the latest batch of lemon wine.	*Door opens, footsteps.* *Bottles clanking, liquid pouring.*
Whitsun:	Look sir, in the corner, that tree – it's covered in bright yellow fruit, what is it?	
Inspector:	A lemon tree my dear Whitsun.	
Narrator:	Suddenly, they heard the sound of a horn in the distance.	*Horn sounds.*
Whitsun:	What was that inspector?	
Inspector:	That'll be part of the job creation scheme for the sound effects engineer.	
Whitsun:	Hang on a minute, who's that man over there?	
Sir L:	Ah yes, that's Roland Butter, manager of the bottling plant.	
Inspector:	In that case Sir Loinsteak, I have reason to believe that it is in this very room that the murders were planned. In fact, I suspect that those bottles of lemon wine are laced!	
Whitsun:	So you think that those white lumps in the wine are lace do you Inspector? Very shrewd.	
Sir L:	This is terrible Inspector.	
Inspector:	What, the script?	
Sir L:	No, not quite that bad. But tell me, who do you suspect as being the perpetrator of this foul deed?	
Inspector:	None other than Roland Butter.	
Sir L:	Roland Butter?	
Whitsun:	Not for me thank you sir, I've just eaten. Besides, we've got a murder to solve.	

Sir L:	But what makes you think that it's Roland?
Inspector:	Well, it's the look in his eye, his unsure stance and the mysterious aura of evil which surrounds him ... but it's mainly the large bag in his hand marked 'the deadliest poison known to man'.
Roland:	It's a fair cop, I'll come clean.
Whitsun:	Here's the soap, you fiend.
Inspector:	But tell me, why did you add the poison to the wine you dastardly villain?
Roland:	Well it's like this: should Sir Loinsteak die, all his money will be shared amongst his servants since he has no living relatives. By killing off the others and then Sir Loinsteak himself, I would inherit the entire fortune.
Inspector:	Gad, it's lucky that we stopped you before you got too far. Take him away from his bottling line, Whitsun, and throw him in jail.
Sir L:	A thousand thanks Inspector Thinkalott. But tell me, how did you possibly deduce that it was Roland who was the murderer?
Inspector:	It was easy Sir Loinsteak, as in all the best mysteries ... the Bottler did it!

*Footsteps.
Roland sobs.*

The End

Birthday Rumblings

THE CAST

Narrator – a narrator
Inspector Thinkalott – a clever detective
Whitsun – his bumbling assistant
Diddit – The Butler
Sir Pentine Lake – a rich toff
Constable Joblot – a police officer
Nick McKaar – a chauffeur

Narrator:	The clock struck midnight at Evening Hall, where the party to celebrate the birthday of Sir Pentine Lake was well under way. It was after only a few hours that Sir Pentine noticed that one of his presents, a gold watch, had gone missing from underneath the brightly decorated birthday tree. He whispered quietly to Diddit, the butler...	*Clock chimes 12.* *Party sounds, glasses, music etc.*
Sir P:	Quick Diddit, summon the police and seal off all the exits.	
Diddit:	Righto Sir... shall I use some of that sealant that we had left over from decorating the scullery?	
Sir P:	What an oaf. Didn't you go to school, stupid?	
Diddit:	Er, yes ... and I came back stupid as well.	
Narrator:	Three minutes later, Inspector Thinkalott's gleaming new five-seater electric police-buggy screeched to a halt outside the hall, having been driven there by his assistant, Whitsun. They had just come from the police station in nearby Letsby Avenue at such a speed that they were out of breath when they approached the door.	*Car screeches to a halt.* *Footsteps.*
Inspector:	Hmmm, you certainly drive like a magician, Whitsun.	
Whitsun:	What do you mean Guv?	
Inspector:	You know, when we were driving along and you turned the car into a side road.	
Narrator:	Without further ado, hesitation or jokes, they rang the bell of Evening Hall.	*Doorbell rings.* *Door opens.*
Inspector:	Evening all.	
Diddit:	That is correct – you must have read the nameplate on the door.	
Narrator:	He entered, followed by Whitsun and three constables. Whitsun had picked these up cheap at an art gallery earlier that afternoon.	*Footsteps.*
Inspector:	What seems to be the problem, Sir Pentine?	

	Sir P:	There's been a robbery Inspector – my gold watch has been stolen, it's worth over one million pounds.
	Inspector:	Hmmm, I deduce that the evil fiend is still somewhere in this very room Sir Pentine – I've got this gut feeling.
	Whitsun:	What do you mean, Inspector – a gut feeling?
Stomach gurgling.	**Inspector:**	<u>Alimentary</u>, my dear Whitsun!
Rustle of paper.	**Narrator:**	Just then, the butler handed the Inspector a mysterious piece of paper.
	Diddit:	Here's a mysterious piece of paper, Inspector.
	Inspector:	Look Whitsun, Diddit's just handed me this.
	Whitsun:	What is it Inspector?
	Inspector:	Er... at first guess, I'd say it was a mysterious piece of paper Whitsun. I'm sorry about Whitsun Sir, he's so daft he thinks Sherlock Holmes is a new housing developer.
	Whitsun:	No guv, I mean what's written on it?
	Inspector:	It's a clue Whitsun. It seems that we're looking for a man with one eye.
	Whitsun:	Wouldn't it be better if we used both eyes Inspector?
	Inspector:	You're right Whitsun. Summon three real constables at once.
Footsteps, door slams, whistles, three gunshots.	**Narrator:**	As the constables arrived, slamming the door behind them, whistles blowing furiously, three shots were fired at the Inspector, Whitsun and the three constables. The first two hurtled past him, the third whistled through his notebook.
Whistling.	**Inspector:**	Why are you whistling through your notebook, Constable?
	Constable:	So we could get a few more gags into the script Inspector.
Breaking glass. Scream.	**Narrator:**	Suddenly, there was the sound of breaking glass and one of the guests, Edna Bucket, screamed loudly.
Footsteps.	**Whitsun:**	Quick, he's escaping through that window.
	Inspector:	Into the cars and fast... Oh no, the battery's flat.
	Whitsun:	What shape should it be, Inspector?
	Constable:	Never fear Inspector Thinkalott, I've just rung the police station and spoken to the radio operator, Colin Allcars, he's sending another vehicle straight away.
	Inspector:	Tell him to send it here instead. Dash it, it's starting to rain.
Car sounds, doors slam, driving off.	**Narrator:**	Another car soon arrived, into which they all piled, speeding off in hot pursuit of the villain. So hot, in fact, that Whitsun had to open a window.

14

Constable:	We'll soon catch him – he's drunk so much beer at the party that he's sure to come to a bitter end.	
Narrator:	Suddenly, as they were driving down a one way street, they saw another vehicle coming straight at them.	*Cars driving.*
Sir P:	Stop that car.	
Narrator:	Whitsun swung the car across the road, forcing the other vehicle to stop. The constable got out and arrested the offending motorist.	*Car sounds, footsteps running, scuffle.*
Constable:	You are charged with driving the wrong way up a one-way street.	
McKarr:	But I was only going one way.	
Constable:	Didn't you see the arrows?	
McKarr:	Arrows? – I didn't even see any archers.	
Sir P:	Good grief, that man is my chauffeur, Nick McKaar.	
Inspector:	There's something else you should know Sir Pentine. That man is also an international criminal. You've had a lucky escape. Look at his wrist, it's your gold watch.	
Sir P:	Gad, so it is.	
Inspector:	I think we'd all better go back to the station and file the charges.	
Narrator:	Whitsun drove them to the police station, hooting the horn vigorously as he approached the car park. Inside, the Scottish Duty Sergeant, Phillip McCup, was pouring them all a nice hot cup of tea.	*Car driving. Car horn sounds. Cup of tea poured.*
Sir P:	I'd just like you to have this as a token of thanks, Inspector, it's a silver comb – a parting gift.	
Inspector:	Thank you Sir, but I must tell you that our services are entirely free. Whitsun what would you say to a little drink?	
Whitsun:	I'd say 'hello little drink'.	
Narrator:	Suddenly, the phone rang.	*Phone rings.*
Constable:	Excuse me Sir Pentine, there's a man on the line wanting to sell you a clothes prop.	
Sir P:	Tell him to hold the line.	
Inspector:	Enough! We've got to go now and solve the mystery of the holdall that keeps emptying its contents all over the road.	
Whitsun:	Have you got any ideas on that one Inspector?	
Inspector:	No Whitsun ... it's an open and shut case.	

The End

Safe Delivery

THE CAST
Narrator – a narrator
Inspector Thinkalott – a clever detective
Whitsun – his bumbling assistant
Anne Ouncer – a station announcer
Guard – a train guard
Kipper – a Sleeping Car Attendant

Crackling fire. *Distant hooting.*	**Narrator:** It was a dark and gloomy night at the police station in the tiny hamlet of Little Doing. Come to mention it, it was a dark and gloomy night in the rest of the hamlet as well, as Inspector Thinkalott and his assistant, Whitsun, settled down for a relaxing evening around the fireside. All was quiet, save for the distant hooting of a very talented bat. Suddenly the phone went.
	Inspector: Go and fetch the phone back Whitsun, it's bound to ring any minute.
Phone rings.	**Narrator:** It did.
	Whitsun: Inspector, it's bad news I'm afraid. The local bank is being robbed.
Distant babble on phone.	**Inspector:** This is terrible, tell them to hold on – we'll be there in ten minutes.
	Whitsun: The manager says he's asked them but the robbers will only hold on for five minutes as they've got a train to catch.
	Inspector: Good grief Whitsun, this could be our first major clue. Let's go to the station.
	Whitsun: But we're already at the station.
Running footsteps, car doors open, engine started.	**Narrator:** Inspector Thinkalott ignored his colleague's comment and led him out into the car park where they leapt into their smart new squad car and quickly turned the engine over.
	Inspector: That's the second time the garage has put the engine in upside-down – I really must have a word with them.
Car drives past.	**Whitsun:** Look boss, there goes their getaway car.
	Inspector: How do you know that, Whitsun?
	Whitsun: It says so in the script, Inspector.
Car driving, tyres screech.	**Narrator:** They arrived at the railway station, tyres screeching on the tarmac, just as the Station Announcer spoke.
	Anne: The train now standing on platform two should really be on the rails. We apologise for any inconvenience caused. The

16

	train now arriving at platform one is the bank robbers' train, calling at Wormwood Scrubs, Pentonville and Dartmoor.	*Train sounds in background.*

Inspector: We must get on that train Whitsun, we must catch them.

Whitsun: Do we need a ticket, Inspector?

Inspector: No, he's innocent – we only want the bank robbers.

Narrator: Several minutes were lost as the robbers and the policemen waited in the queue to buy their tickets. Then, Inspector Thinkalott remembered that he had brought their recently-purchased season tickets with them and they went straight to the train, beating the robbers on board by three minutes. *Footsteps, station noises.*

Anne: Will the passengers who have just taken the 10.45 train to Glasgow, kindly return it to the station.

Narrator: The train steamed out of the station (which was strange really, as it was diesel powered), with Inspector Thinkalott, Whitsun and the robbers safely on board. *Train chugging.*

Guard: Tickets please.

Narrator: The two policemen gave in their season tickets and told the guard what had happened.

Guard: We must make sure nobody leaves the train.

Whitsun: Why's that?

Guard: It gets rather lonely at night.

Inspector: My guess is that they've hidden in the sleeping car, let's take a look.

Whitsun: Look sir, there's the Sleeping Car Attendant. *Snoring.*

Inspector: Wake him up then.

Whitsun: Wake up. The Inspector wants a few words with you.

Kipper: Er...Um...I'm afraid I can't see you at the moment Inspector.

Inspector: Try opening your eyes.

Kipper: Ah. that's better. Anyway, Inspector, I don't know where the bank robbers have gone.

Whitsun: Hold on a minute ... that little room in the corner ... what is it Inspector?

Inspector: It's a toilet.

Whitsun: Gosh, how did you deduce that sir?

Inspector: A lavatory, my dear Whitsun.

Narrator: It was then that the Inspector noticed something strange and, turning to the Attendant once more, he spoke.

Inspector:	Just a second, haven't I seen your face somewhere else?
Kipper:	I don't think so; it's always been on the front of my head.
Inspector:	But it's that hair ... that nose ... that head, shoulders, knees and toes, knees and toes.
ALL:	(SINGING)... and eyes and ears and mouth and nose...
Inspector:	Shut up, Shut up! I accuse you of being one of the bank robbers, you fiend.
Guard:	Gasp! How do you know that Inspector?
Inspector:	It was simple. If he was asleep all the time, he would have known nothing of the robbery. That, coupled with the fact that he's still wearing a stocking over his head led me to deduce that this is our man.
Whitsun:	But where are the rest of the gang, Inspector?
Inspector:	Hiding behind that large bank safe at the end of the corridor, I presume.
Guard:	Brilliant, Inspector – another case solved. What will you do now?
Inspector:	Well, first, we've got to go to the Ritzy Hotel – they've had a bad case of poisoning.
Whitsun:	At least it'll make a change from the bad case of claret they had last week!
Inspector:	And then we've got to go and solve the mystery of the old lady who keeps giving away thousands of pounds of fake money.
Whitsun:	Counterfeit?
Inspector:	Of course I did Whitsun – she had two.

The End

18

The Thief of Battree Farm

THE CAST
Narrator – a narrator
Inspector Thinkalott – a clever detective
Whitsun – his bumbling assistant
Farmer Lottacorn – a farmer
Benny – the farm hand
Lottie Bottle – the milk maid

Narrator:	The mist swirled across the moors as dusk fell over Battree Farm. Farmer Lottacorn heaved a heavy sigh as he finished putting the last of his animals to bed for the night. It had been an unusually long day, since his watch had stopped working several weeks ago, and he was feeling very tired. He turned and spoke to his farm hand, Benny, as they walked from the horses' stables towards the cottage.	*Wind howling.* *Assorted animal noises.* *Footsteps.*
Farmer:	Well, that's the animals locked up for the night, Benny. How about a nice cup of cocoa back in the farmhouse?	
Benny:	Ooh arr, that'd be great, Farmer Lottacorn, Surr. Did you remember the sheep, by the way?	*Sheep baa.*
Farmer:	Don't be daft – sheep don't like cocoa. Besides, my wife would never allow them to sit on her new sofa.	
Narrator:	They entered through the creaky door of the cottage and sat down in front of the fire. Suddenly, there was a noise.	*Door creaks open.* *Any clunking noise!*
Farmer:	Wasn't that a noise I just heard coming from over there, Benny?	
Benny:	Yes, Surr, that be the sound effects man.	
Farmer:	No, you fool. I mean coming from next door – listen.	
Narrator:	The farmer heard the noise again, and so, the two men crept towards the door and peered cautiously round.	*The same clunking noise!*
Farmer:	Arr, it's only Rover, the cat – but look on the mantelpiece! My gold ring was there when we went out and now it's gone. That ring is worth thousands of pounds – I'm going to call the police.	
Benny:	What are you going to call them?	
Narrator:	The farmer ignored Benny and summoned the police, whose car squelched to a halt in the muddy drive some minutes later. It was Inspector Thinkalott of Scotland Yard and his assistant, Whitsun. The Inspector knocked on the door and the farmer opened it.	*Car skids to a halt.* *Footsteps.* *Knock on door.* *Door opens.*
Inspector:	Farmer Lottacorn?	

	Farmer:	No, not much – I'm afraid it's been a bad harvest this year, but do come in anyway.
Footsteps.	Inspector:	Thank you. I tried the bell but there was no ring.
	Farmer:	That's right, it's been stolen – it happened while Benny, my farm hand, and I were locking up for the night. There was only one other person in the house at the time apart from my good wife, and that was Lottie Bottle, the milk maid.
	Inspector:	Bring her in here and I will question her.
Footsteps.	Narrator:	The girl was called into the room and the Inspector began the questioning.
	Inspector:	Where were you at the time of the crime, my dear girl?
	Lottie:	Upstairs in my room, Inspector.
	Whitsun:	There you are Inspector – that rules her out completely.
	Inspector:	You buffoon, Whitsun – don't you realise that the guilty party is bound to lie?
	Narrator:	The Inspector then realised that, whilst he had been questioning Lottie, someone had slipped out of the room.
	Inspector:	Someone's slipped out of the room!
Squelching noise.	Whitsun:	Ah, that must have been because of all that mud we brought in from the drive, Inspector.
	Inspector:	Silence, Whitsun. Where's your hand, Farmer?
	Farmer:	Why, it was on the end of my arm a few moments ago Inspector, but I'll have a check and see ...
	Inspector:	I mean your farm hand. I thought there was something odd about him when I noticed that his hand seemed to be covered in some strange sediment. An important discovery – we must act fast.
	Whitsun:	Why, Inspector?
	Inspector:	Because this play is running late. Let the chase commence!
	Whitsun:	After you, Farmer Lottacorn.
	Inspector:	No, Whitsun, we're not after the Farmer – he's innocent. We're after the farm hand.
	Farmer:	I can't believe it – Benny, a thief! – He must have sneaked off and stolen the ring whilst I was locking up the animals.
Running footsteps. *Sizzling sound.*	Narrator:	The chase began with the Inspector, Whitsun and the farmer running hot-foot after the farm hand. Their feet were so hot, in fact, that they had to continue the chase barefoot. Suddenly the farmer ran into the farmhouse, to emerge a few seconds later.

Farmer:	Quick, over here – he's been trapped in the farmhouse.	
Inspector:	How's the milk maid?	
Farmer:	We get it out of our flock of cows every morning.	*Cows moo.*
Inspector:	You mean herd. Herd of cows.	
Whitsun:	Yes, it's a little village on the Isle of Wight, Inspector.	
Narrator:	It soon became clear to the somewhat confused Inspector that Lottie had been the hero of the day by capturing Benny as he had run back into the cottage to hide, unaware of her presence.	
Inspector:	Well done Lottie, we're proud of you. How did you do it?	
Lottie:	It's quite simple, Inspector. You see, I've been taking macramé lessons at evening classes.	
Inspector:	Macramé? I thought that was some sort of fancy raffia-work – how could that help you apprehend this villain?	
Lottie:	I just hit him over the head with this great big text book.	
Inspector:	Brilliant. Right, Whitsun – you tie him up and I'll call for assistance.	*Rope tying sound(!).*
Whitsun:	What with, Inspector?	
Inspector:	The telephone, of course.	
Whitsun:	How can I tie him up with a telephone?	
Farmer:	This is all very well, Inspector, but what about my gold ring?	
Inspector:	Walk this way, Farmer Lottacorn.	*Footsteps.*
Narrator:	They walked that way towards the horse trough, where the Inspector pointed to a bright, shiny object sticking out of the mud at the bottom of the trough.	
Whitsun:	Golly, how did you deduce that the ring would be there, Inspector?	
Inspector:	<u>Sedimentary</u>, my dear Whitsun. It was the sludge on Benny's hand that gave it away – the horse trough is an obvious place to hide things to be collected later. It appears that he planned to retrieve it when the coast was clear.	
Whitsun:	You mean he was going to smuggle it out to sea, Inspector?	
Inspector:	Quiet, Whitsun, we have to go now and solve the mystery of the disappearing information kiosk.	
Whitsun:	How's it going, Inspector?	
Inspector:	Well, the police no longer have anyone to help them with their enquiries...	

The End

The Man who came into the Cold

<u>**THE CAST**</u>
Narrator – a narrator
Inspector Thinkalott – a clever detective
Whitsun – his bumbling assistant
Minnit – the waiter
Edna Nuvven – the manageress
Deepan – the pizza chef
Mustapha Lager – a restaurateur

Footsteps.	Narrator:	Inspector Thinkalott and his assistant, Whitsun, of Scotland Yard entered the bistro looking forward to an evening away from the bustle of the police station...
	Inspector:	Well, here we are, Whitsun.
	Whitsun:	Brilliant deduction, Inspector – I wish I was as clever as you.
	Inspector:	You should be – you did alright at school didn't you?
	Whitsun:	I did well at everything except lessons. But you must admit, if I'm not bright, at least I'm a safe driver.
	Inspector:	That's true, although quite why you like driving safes beats me. Anyway, I hope you're going to behave once we're inside – I've heard that you've been thrown out of more restaurants than you've had hot dinners.
Sneezing.	Narrator:	Just then, Whitsun spotted Minnit, the waiter, and caught his eye – it had dropped out when he sneezed – and beckoned to him.
	Minnit:	Good evening, gentlemen, welcome to our little bistro. Would you like to take a seat?
	Whitsun:	No thanks – we've plenty back at the station.
	Inspector:	Shut up, Whitsun, he means sit down and choose your meal.
Chairs scrape on floor. *Water sound.* *Paper rustles.*	Narrator:	The two detectives sat down and pored over the menu. The waiter patiently mopped it up and began to write down their order.
	Inspector:	We'd like two extra-large meals but we're a bit short of cash – can you give us a quote?
	Minnit:	Certainly sir – 'To be, or not to be, that is the question – Whether 'tis nobler in the mind...'
	Inspector:	Alright, forget the money side of it, just bring us the food.
	Minnit:	Would you like a starter, sir?
	Inspector:	Yes please. How about you, Whitsun?
	Whitsun:	I'll have a carburettor instead.

22

Narrator:	The waiter walked away and turned into the kitchen – which was a pretty neat trick, all in all – leaving Whitsun and Thinkalott to study the wine list. Just then Edna Nuvven, the manageress of the restaurant, appeared – an even better trick than the turning into a kitchen routine – and seemed to be in a bit of a state.	*Footsteps.*
Edna:	Help, help... there's a human body in my freezer!	
Inspector:	Gad. Whitsun, what would you make of that?	
Whitsun:	A kebab, perhaps, or a nice stew – maybe even a tasty bolognaise...	
Inspector:	May we be of service, madam?	
Edna:	Ah, you look like two undercover plainclothes off-duty policemen – just what I need.	
Inspector:	I'm Inspector Thinkalott.	
Deepan:	Thinkalott of the Yard?	
Whitsun:	Well, the metric system does have its advantages but you can't really beat good old feet and inches.	
Narrator:	They walked into the kitchen, opened the freezer and peered in.	*Footsteps. Door opens.*
Whitsun:	What's he doing in there, Inspector?	
Deepan:	Shivering, I would imagine.	*Chattering teeth.*
Inspector:	You'll have to give him artificial respiration, Whitsun. No, on second thoughts, this is serious – better give him the real thing.	
Whitsun:	There's no need for that, look – he's moving. We'll turn the freezer off and thaw him out. Then we'll soon find out what's going on. After all, it's not every day that you find a body in your freezer.	*Rustling of packages.*
Edna:	Ooh, look, part of his upper stomach's frozen solid.	
Inspector:	Ah yes, that's because it's a chest freezer.	
Narrator:	All was silent in the kitchen, as they waited for the body to defrost, save for the gentle clinking of glasses and rattling of spoons, caused by an under-used sound effects engineer who was sitting in the corner of the room. The Inspector confused the poor fellow by breaking the silence.	*Clinking glasses, rattling spoons.* *Crash!*
Inspector:	Hmm – I smell a rat.	
Deepan:	Ah, it must be done, I'll take it out of the oven.	
Whitsun:	I can smell something strange too, it must be the fish defrosting in the freezer. Tell me, Edna, how do you stop fish smelling?	

Edna:	You cut off their noses.
Inspector:	Quiet everybody, he's coming round.
Whitsun:	Excuse me, Inspector, but would you mind if I nipped off to the toilet?
Inspector:	This is ridiculous. If everybody went off to the toilet at a time like this, then where would we be?
Whitsun:	In the toilet, I guess.
Narrator:	Just then, the Narrator spoke, as if to point out the fact that he hadn't said anything for several minutes.
Inspector:	Wait a minute...
Minnit:	Yes sir?

Inspector:	No, no, I mean look – in the man's hand. It looks like it might very well be a bottle of that deadly poison which travels around the intestines, into the stomach and eats away people's insides.
Whitsun:	Gosh. How did you identify it. Inspector?
Inspector:	<u>Alimentary</u>, my dear Whitsun.
Narrator:	The man gradually opened his mouth and spoke.
Lager:	Arrgh. Th-thank you, th-thank you v-very m-much f-for releasing me. I must have been in there f-for hours.
Edna:	Just a moment, Inspector – I recognise him now... it's Mustapha Lager, the manager of the curry shop on the other side of the road. You may need assistance, officers, he's a very violent man. But I'm afraid we don't have a phone here – can you telephone from your car?
Whitsun:	Of course we can – a phone's got buttons and a twisty lead, whilst a car's much larger and has a wheel at each corner.
Inspector:	We don't need help. He'll not resist us as he's already injured – he's got a broken nose.
Whitsun:	Gosh, Inspector, how can you tell that from here?
Inspector:	Simple, it's running with a limp.
Whitsun:	Come clean, you fiend – we've caught you red-handed.
Lager:	Alright, alright. I admit it – I was trying to poison the restaurant's food last night, but I accidentally fell in the deep freeze and got shut in.
Edna:	But why did you want to poison the food?
Lager:	Simple – your restaurant is far too popular, nobody wants to eat in mine anymore and I'm going bankrupt.

24

Whitsun:	You won't need money where you're going, you fiend, thanks to the Inspector.
Narrator:	The villain was whisked away and locked up and Thinkalott and Whitsun were invited to a celebration party at the bistro the following evening, where the drinks flowed freely.
Minnit:	Excuse me, Inspector, but your glass is empty – would you like another one?
Inspector:	What would I do with another empty glass?
Edna:	I'd just like to say a few words to thank you, Inspector, for saving the future of this bistro. We really are indebted to you and Whitsun.
ALL:	That's right – hear, hear – good old Thinkalott...
Deepan:	Tell me, sirs, what are you going to do with your time, now that you've cleared up this little mystery?
Inspector:	Well, we've got to look into the mysterious disappearance of all of the lavatories in the police station.
Deepan:	Really? How's the investigation doing?
Inspector:	Not too well – we've got nothing to go on at the moment...

Footsteps. Scuffle.

Drinks, glasses, party sounds.

The End

All at Sea

THE CAST

Narrator – a narrator
Inspector Thinkalott – a clever detective
Whitsun – his bumbling assistant
Lucy Lastick – a market trader
Captain Scarfe – a seafaring captain
One-eyed Jim – his first mate
Bus conductor – a conductor of buses
Monsieur Duvet – a French fellow

Seagulls, waves crashing on beach.	**Narrator:** Inspector Thinkalott and his assistant, Whitsun, were taking a break from the rigours of crime busting and were relaxing on a beach. The tide had come in some three hours previously, unknown to them, as they were lazily looking <u>through</u> the newspapers.
Newspaper rustle.	
	Whitsun: Bit thin, these newspapers – I can see through them to the pier. No, I tell a lie, it's only a Lord of the Manor.
	Inspector: I see here that there's been a lot of smuggling in these parts recently – it seems that some crooks are smuggling stolen jewels into this country from France by hiding them inside melons. It's lucky that we can keep a low profile and really enjoy our holiday inconspicuously, eh Whitsun?
Police siren.	**Whitsun:** That's right sir. Oh, and shall I turn the car's siren and flashing blue lights off, now we've been parked on the beach for a few hours?
Footsteps.	**Narrator:** After a while, they decided to go for a walk to find a boat for a cruise around the harbour but were having problems trying to follow their map.
	Inspector: Quick, follow that map, Whitsun ... it's getting away.
Lorry drives off.	**Whitsun:** I told you not to glue it to the back of that lorry, sir. Dash it – it's no use Inspector, we'll never find our way now.
Footsteps.	**Narrator:** They wandered off and decided to take a bus rather than trust their own sense of direction.
	Whitsun: Does this bus stop at the harbour?
	Bus Cond: If it doesn't, there'll be a heck of a splash. Ho, ho, ho.
Bus driving. It stops, footsteps. Boat engine chugs.	**Narrator:** The bus whisked them right to where the boat was leaving for a remote and distant isle.
	Captain: All aboard! All aboard! Ha harrrr.
	Inspector: Quick, Whitsun, let's catch this boat.
	Whitsun: I don't think my butterfly net is big enough, sir.

26

Captain:	Ha haaar ... are you aboard, my lad?
Whitsun:	No, sir – I'm a police officer. A board is short and thick.
Inspector:	Pipe down. Whitsun, and try to behave.
Captain:	Welcome aboard, me hearties. My name's Scarfe – but you can call me Cap'n.
Inspector:	Cap'n Scarfe?
Captain:	Thanks for offering, but I've got my own. Let me introduce my first mate, one-eyed Jim. Ha haaar.
Jim:	Welcome aboard, ha haaar – we'll soon be on the island. I hope you enjoy your little trip.
Whitsun:	So do I – whenever I've been on a ferry before, it's made me cross.
Inspector:	Very droll, Whitsun. Just concentrate on not getting seasick.
Jim:	If you're worried, have a nice glass of milk to drink and it'll settle your stomach.
Narrator:	One-eyed Jim brought out two large tumblers of milk, which he gingerly placed upon the table.
Jim:	Your milk, sir.
Whitsun:	No, I'm not – I've already told you, I'm a policeman.
Narrator:	Just as the two glasses were placed on the table, they exploded with an almighty bang.
Inspector:	I think the milk's gone off.
Whitsun:	Gad – do you think someone's trying to kill us, Inspector?
Inspector:	Could be, Whitsun. At least we've reached the safety of the island – let's get off and try to find out who could have sent that explosive milk on board.
Narrator:	They wandered around the island, admiring the scenery, until they chanced upon a quaint little stall, set up in the shade of a clump of trees, and run by a sweet young lady by the name of Lucy. They decided to buy a few souvenirs to take back to their chums at the station.
Lucy:	Greetings, and welcome to my stall, my friends. Feast your eyes upon the treasures on my table.
Whitsun:	Hmmm ... not bad – but tell me, what's in that big chest in the corner?
Lucy:	Ah – you'd like to look at my chest, would you?
Inspector:	Not while we're on duty, ma'am. But we'd like to take a look in that trunk.

Glasses clink.

Glasses clink.
Explosion.

Footsteps.

27

	Lucy:	I'm afraid that's out of the question, sir, nothing in there is for sale.
	Inspector:	But it's got 'cheapo souvenirs, positively not smuggled jewellery' written on the lid.
	Lucy:	That's just er ... souvenirs I buy from Monsieur Duvet in France and export for sale on the mainland. I just keep them all in there for safe keeping.
Sound of something thrown into air and back to ground (eg whistling).	Narrator:	As she spoke, Inspector Thinkalott quickly cast his eye up into the trees above them.
	Inspector:	I'm glad you caught my eye, Whitsun, can you see what I can up there in that oak tree?
	Whitsun:	Cripes! It can't be...?
	Inspector:	Quite right, Whitsun, it isn't. In fact, it appears to be a number of large yellow fruit, nestling in the branches above us. What's more, I believe that they are the very same fruit which contain the smuggled jewels.
	Whitsun:	Golly, Inspector, how did you deduce that?
	Inspector:	<u>A-melon-in-tree</u>, my dear Whitsun. What's more – in an oak tree!
Footsteps.	Narrator:	Just then, One-eyed Jim scuttled on the scene.
	Whitsun:	How dare you scuttle in front of the Inspector.
	Jim:	I'm sorry, was it his turn?
	Inspector:	Enough! One-eyed Jim, I have reason to believe that it is you, along with Lucy Lastick here, who are the smugglers.
Footsteps.	Duvet:	Hold it right there – my name is Monsieur Duvet.
	Inspector:	That can't be your real name.
	Duvet:	You're right – Duvet is only a cover. But don't move – this melon here is loaded.
	Inspector:	Cripes – an exploding melon!
	Duvet:	Yes, say your last words, Inspector.
	Inspector:	Cripes – an exploding melon!
Table lifted and moved. Groans.	Narrator:	Suddenly, Whitsun grabbed one of the stall's trestle tables and swiftly rotated it, knocking Lucy, One-eyed Jim and Monsieur Duvet into a crumpled heap.
	Whitsun:	There, that's turned the tables on you, you fiends. Cap'n Scarfe is waiting on his disguised police launch to take you to jail on the mainland – he's really a detective and suspected you all along, but he just needed to find the evidence.

28

Inspector: Clever work, Whitsun. But tell me, Jim, I couldn't help noticing that you've got two eyes – so why do they call you One-eyed Jim?

Jim: Simple – it's because there's only one 'i' in Jim! Ha harr.

Inspector: Just as I suspected. Come hither, Whitsun, our holiday is nearly over and we must get back to help our colleagues solve the mystery of the missing saucepan cleaning pads.

Whitsun: Any ideas on that one, Inspector?

Inspector: No, Whitsun, but the police are scouring the area.

The End

Mystery on the Mountain

THE CAST
Narrator – a narrator
Inspector Thinkalott – a clever detective
Whitsun – his bumbling assistant
Carrie Beener – a hiker
Mike Umpass – an English villain

Barking sound. *Jet planes passing.* *Explosions.* *Footsteps.*	**Narrator:** All was quiet on the hillside, except for the gentle barking of a rather confused rabbit, the frequent roar from the engines of passing Royal Air Force jets and the constant rumble of the explosions at the nearby quarry. Inspector Thinkalott of Scotland Yard and his bumbling assist- ant, Whitsun, were enjoying a well-deserved break from crime-busting by hiking up Britain's highest mountain, Ben Nevis.
	Inspector: Tiring stuff, this. Don't you agree, Whitsun?
	Whitsun: You bet, Inspector.
	Inspector: Well, I used to put the odd pound or two on the horses or into a fruit machine. Tell me, Whitsun, have you ever dabbled on a horse?
	Whitsun: Only once but the trainer made me mop it up.
	Narrator: Suddenly, as if from nowhere, there was a high-pitched whistle.
High pitched whistle.	**Whitsun:** Look what I've found on the ground, Inspector – it's a nice, shiny, high-pitched whistle.
Dog barking.	**Inspector:** It must have been dropped by that woman up there with her dog. It's no use to us, put it down.
	Whitsun: Why should we put the dog down, Guv? It hasn't done us any harm.
Footsteps. *Mumbled voice.* *Shuffling feet.*	**Narrator:** They quickened their pace and soon caught up with the woman and gave her back the whistle. The woman mumbled her thanks, somewhat dejectedly as she continued to shuffle along the pathway.
	Inspector: You're looking down, madam.
	Carrie: I have to, otherwise I trip over all these rocks.
	Inspector: What I mean, madam, is that you're looking a trifle upset.
	Carrie: Hang on. I'll just wipe the custard, jelly and sponge from my hair.
	Whitsun: Something *must* have upset you to have poured your packed lunch over your head, if you don't mind me saying so.
	Carrie: You're right. Something terrible is happening to the

	mountain. Have you noticed all those hikers with their rucsacs bulging with huge rocks that they've taken from the top of the mountain?	*Clunking of rocks.*
Whitsun:	What are they up to?	
Carrie:	Oh, about four thousand feet.	
Narrator:	Carrie Beena, for it was her, sat down with the two policemen and they discussed the strange goings-on as the Inspector opened his trusty flask and poured them all a mug of his favourite brew.	*Drinks pouring.*
Whitsun:	What is this peculiar, tangy beverage, Inspector?	
Inspector:	A lemon tea, my dear Whitsun.	
Narrator:	As they sat there, they noticed several of the heavily laden hikers moving down the hill.	*Footsteps on gravel.*
Inspector:	We must get to the bottom of this, Whitsun.	
Whitsun:	But we were trying to get to the top.	
Inspector:	What I mean is that we must go under cover.	
Whitsun:	Great! Lucky for me I brought my Laura Ashley continental duvet.	
Inspector:	There'll be no sleeping on this mission – we must be brave and fearless. What are you doing curled up in a ball amongst the rocks, Whitsun?	
Whitsun:	I'm trying to be a little bolder.	
Inspector:	That's given me an idea – see those hikers having their lunch over there? We could get rid of the rocks in their rucsacs and hide in them to find out what's going on.	
Carrie:	Gosh! You're so brave. You just have to be policemen.	
Inspector:	It's okay, madam, we already are.	
Narrator:	With that they secretively hurled the boulders from the rucsacs of the two hikers and climbed inside. It was later that week when all was quiet that the two managed to peer from under the flaps of the rucsacs.	*More rocks clunking.*
Whitsun:	I don't believe it – all that time and we're still halfway up a mountain. What's going on, Inspector?	
Inspector:	I've got a fair idea, Whitsun, but we'd never get the big wheel or the coconut shy up here. But seriously – look at that man, the one issuing instructions to the hikers.	
Mike:	Righto, men, dump the rocks on top of this pile here. We'll soon have finished our cunning and dastardly plan. Heh, heh.	*Yet more rocks clunking.*
Narrator:	On hearing this, the two policemen leapt out and	

Footsteps.	approached the bearded man in a bobble hat.
	Inspector: Curses, I wish we could get out of this bobble hat as easily as the rucsac... You there. You're under arrest. Don't deny your guilt or try to get away, you'll soon be caught by my blonde-haired assistant.
	Mike: It's a fair cop.
	Inspector: Remove your false beard, you fiend, and reveal yourself.
	Whitsun: Cripes! It's Mike Umpass – the world's greatest hiker and leader of the Mountain Liberation Front.
	Inspector: Okay then, Mike. We want to know precisely what you're up to. It's time to spill the beans.
	Whitsun: Too late, sir, Carrie did that just before the incident with the trifle.
	Mike: Sigh. I knew we'd never get away with it. We were determined to make Scafell Pike the tallest mountain in Great Britain, rather than that Scottish place, Ben Nevis.
	Inspector: I knew it. You've been reducing the height of Ben Nevis and adding the boulders from it to the summit of this mountain, Scafell Pike.
	Mike: And we'd have succeeded too, if it wasn't for you and your bumbling assistant.
Snoring, yawning.	**Whitsun:** I've been up most mountains, you know. I've also hiked along the Pennine Way, Hadrian's Wall, along the South Coastal path and a fair bit of the North Yorkshire Moors, not to mention a few days wandering along Offa's Dyke...
	Inspector: You'll have to forgive Whitsun – he tends to ramble.
Clattering of handcuffs.	**Narrator:** With that, the policemen slapped the handcuffs on the mountain-napper and made a quick call from the conveniently situated public call box. The leader of the local Mountain Rescue Team duly arrived with his chums and the task of replacing the stolen rocks began in earnest.
	Whitsun: Here, take this trumpet, you scoundrel.
Trumpet sounds.	**Mike:** Whatever for?
	Whitsun: So that you can accompany us all the way to the station.
	Inspector: So much for a quiet away-from-it-all holiday. Anyway, we'd better lock this fiend up and get back to work. Remind me, Whitsun, how are we getting on with the great big hole that's appeared in the fence around the local nudist camp?
	Whitsun: Don't worry sir, I'm looking into it.

The End

Tunnel Vision

THE CAST
Narrator – a narrator
Inspector Thinkalott – a clever detective
Whitsun – his bumbling assistant
Voice – a voice on a radio
Montague – a passer-by
Brian – a barman
Lydia Dustbin – a mysterious lady

Narrator:	Inspector Thinkalott and his bumbling assistant, Superintendent Whitsun, were relaxing at the police station, drinking cocoa in their uniform duffel coats.	*Slurping sounds.*
Whitsun:	I wish we could afford cups, Inspector – these duffel coats make my cocoa terribly hairy.	
Narrator:	Just then, the phone rang.	*Phone rings.*
Inspector:	Answer the phone, Whitsun.	
Whitsun:	But I didn't understand the question, guv.	
Inspector:	What's the news, Whitsun?	
Whitsun:	It's the boring bit after Neighbours has finished, but that's not important right now. Come on, we have an appointment on the south coast.	
Narrator:	They got in their car and sped off.	*Car doors and driving off.*
Inspector:	Turn the radio on, Whitsun.	
Whitsun:	But I don't think it fancies me, sir.	
Inspector:	Attention Whisky, Whisky, Tango.	*Crackling radio.*
Voice:	Whisky, Whisky, Tango … understood – that's one Tango and a double Scotch. And is that with or without fries?	
Narrator:	The Inspector abandoned his attempts to use the radio and, before long. they found themselves in a deserted field on the south coast. Suddenly an old man appeared.	*Car stops. Footsteps.*
Montague:	I'm so glad you've arrived. It's the Channel Tunnel.	
Whitsun:	What Channel Tunnel?	
Montague:	Precisely – it's been stolen.	
Whitsun:	Gasp.	
Inspector:	Tell me, where was it?	
Montague:	It used to start right here, until this morning, that is – I was taking my dog for a walk …	*Dog barks.*
Whitsun:	Aah, what a lovely doggie. What's his name?	

	Montague:	I call him Handyman.
	Whitsun:	Why's that?
	Montague:	Because he's always doing odd jobs around the house. Anyway, I was out walking when suddenly I couldn't believe my eyes.
	Inspector:	Neither can I sir – have they always been large, purple and furry?
Footsteps. Pub sounds.	Narrator:	The two detectives decided to pursue their inquiries in the public bar of the Yak and Tapeworm.
	Whitsun:	Excuse me, is the bar tender here?
	Brian:	No – it's made of wood, see.
	Inspector:	He means is the barman here?
	Brian:	Oh, I see. That's me, then.
	Inspector:	Tell me, stout yeoman, have you by any chance spotted anyone in here carrying an exceedingly large tunnel.
	Brian:	Hmmm ... tricky one, that ... let me see ... we had a fellow with a suspension bridge in here last Tuesday but no tunnels I'm afraid.
	Whitsun:	Isn't this getting like a church's Christmas fancy cake and pudding sale, Inspector?
	Inspector:	You mean a 'trifle bizarre', Whitsun? Yes it is – but I do feel that we're getting close to solving this crime. Let's see if we can find some clues.
Running footsteps.	Whitsun:	The locals look innocent enough, guv, but look, the woman who was drinking whisky in the corner has just run out.
	Inspector:	Well, buy her another one then, if it bothers you.
	Whitsun:	No, Inspector, she took one look at us and left the pub.
Glasses smash, footsteps. Knock on door, door opens.	Narrator:	They knocked some glasses to the floor, partly in their haste to follow the woman and partly to give the sound effects person something to do. They knocked at a rundown building and an old man opened the door in his pyjamas.
	Whitsun:	That's a funny place to have a door, Inspector.
	Inspector:	Never mind that, we've lost our quarry.
	Whitsun:	Wasn't it a tunnel we're looking for, not a quarry?
	Inspector:	Look – she must have gone through one of those doors.
	Whitsun:	But which one, Inspector?
Door opens.	Narrator:	The Inspector wasted no time at all and, ignoring the brown and blue doors, chose the yellow one and, once through it, they spotted an unbelievably large hole.

Whitsun:	Gad – we've found the tunnel, Inspector. How did you know which door to choose?	
Inspector:	A yellow entry, my dear Whitsun. Anyway, let's commandeer this handy train and find out where the tunnel comes out – it's only 20 miles long.	*Train noise.*
Narrator:	It was three days later that they arrived at the other end, following a combination of leaves on the track, staff shortages and a delay in the supply of the special fluid that is wiped on sandwiches to make them stiff and curly.	
Inspector:	Unless I'm very much mistaken, Whitsun, we must have come up under the National Midwestleys Bank in Sittingbourne.	
Whitsun:	Fantastic, sir! How did you work that out?	
Inspector:	It says so on that little brass plaque up there.	
Narrator:	Suddenly, a huge metal cupboard filled with gold bars dropped from the roof of the tunnel and crashed into a waiting trolley.	*Crashing noise.*
Whitsun:	That looks like a safe landing, sir.	
Inspector:	Yes indeed – but, more importantly, look who's up there.	
Whitsun:	It's the mysterious lady!	
Inspector:	Quick, Whitsun, follow me.	*Footsteps.*
Narrator:	They approached the lady and formally arrested her.	
Lydia:	What do you mean, you're arresting me? What's the charge?	
Whitsun:	Oh, there's no charge, madam, it's all part of the service.	
Inspector:	I charge you with stealing the Tunnel, placing it under this bank vault in Kent and pinching its gold.	
Whitsun:	What a brilliant deduction, Inspector. But tell me, how did she possibly manage to steal a tunnel?	
Inspector:	Since a tunnel is just a weightless hole in the ground consisting of air, it was a simple matter to sneak it away during the night in carrier bags and balloons.	
Lydia:	You've got me bang to rights, officer. It's a fair cop. I'm as sick as a parrot.	
Inspector:	Now, come with us back to the station and we'll take a statement then, and we'll get back to work. Remember, we've got to help the murder squad drag the reservoir.	
Whitsun:	How's it going, Inspector?	
Inspector:	Well, they've managed to drag it as far as Leeds but they're getting a bit out of breath.	

The End

Trophy Trouble

THE CAST

Narrator – a narrator
Inspector Thinkalott – a clever detective
Whitsun – his bumbling assistant
Mashee Niblick - the Golf Course Manager
Beatrix - the bar lady
Sergeant Sergent - a sergeant

Birds tweeting, sheep bleating, road drills.	Narrator:	Whitsun was enjoying a peaceful day at the police station in the country town of Little Doing. The birds were tweeting merrily, the sheep were bleating happily and the workmen outside were drilling joyfully. His Governor, Inspector Thinkalott, was out of the office on a course for a few days, and Whitsun was left holding the fort.
	Whitsun:	Dashed heavy, this fort, Sergeant. I wish I could put it down.
	Sergeant:	No problem, sir – I know a good vet.
	Narrator:	The peace was soon broken
Phone rings.	Sergeant:	The phone's ringing, sir.
Water sloshing.	Whitsun:	Maybe we shouldn't have put it in that bucket of water. Quick, dry it out and answer it.
	Narrator:	Whitsun was soon speaking with Inspector Thinkalott.
	Whitsun:	Which course did you say you were on sir?
	Inspector:	Gleneagles. Listen, Whitsun, I need you to join me up here.
	Whitsun:	Why – which bit of you has fallen off?
	Inspector:	No, you fool – get the first train to Scotland and meet me here.
	Whitsun:	That's impossible sir ... the first train to Scotland was in the mid-19th century – I think I've missed it.
Car driving. Door opens and closes, footsteps.	Narrator:	It wasn't until the following day that Whitsun arrived by taxi at the golf course.
	Whitsun:	Sorry I'm late, but I forgot to put my clock back.
	Inspector:	But the clocks didn't go back last night.
	Whitsun:	No – I forgot to put my clock back in the bedroom, I left it in the kitchen.
	Inspector:	Let me introduce the Manager of the golf course to you, a Mr. Mashee Niblick.
	Narrator:	The introductions took place and the Manager outlined the problem.

Mashee:	Someone's gorn and stolen all the bally trophies from the trophy cabinet. Worth thousands of pounds, see, and we can't afford that sort of loss – we're a bit short of cash. Look – they even stole a rare statue of our founder, Glen Eagle – it was an enormous bust.	
Whitsun:	Hmmm ... tell me, sir, have you anything to go on?	
Mashee:	Just this lavatory.	*Loo flushes.*
Whitsun:	I mean, are there any clues?	
Inspector:	Only this large, old piece of half-unravelled string – do you think it'll be of any use?	
Whitsun:	<u>A frayed knot,</u> Inspector.	
Inspector:	I can see that, you fool. Never mind, let's nip over to the far end of the golf course.	
Whitsun:	Is it a fairway?	
Inspector:	Not really, but we'll take a buggy just in case. But first, we'd better disguise ourselves as golfers, so we can melt into the background.	
Narrator:	Before long, the two detectives arrived on the green, resplendent in Rupert-Bear style trousers, colourful jumpers and exceedingly silly flat caps.	*Electric engine noises.*
Inspector:	That's a very bright jersey you've got on, Whitsun.	
Whitsun:	Yes sir ... they'd run out of stupid Friesians. Hold on while I dislodge it from my shoulders ...	*Cow moos.*
Inspector:	Now, if we're to look like golfers we'll need to start playing a bit of golf. Pass me an iron, Whitsun.	
Whitsun:	This is no time for domestic chores, Guv. Look, what's that over there, in that large sand pit?	
Inspector:	Sand, I do believe.	
Whitsun:	Next to that – it looks like a small yellow golfing tee, Inspector.	
Narrator:	They hurried over to the bunker, where they stood staring into the sand-filled pit. Unperturbed, Whitsun calmly combed his hair.	
Inspector:	I do wish you'd have left that small rabbit-like animal at home, Whitsun - and stop combing it.	
Narrator:	Whitsun reluctantly put the hare on the ground and watched, amazed, as it started burrowing into the sand.	*Digging sound.*
Whitsun:	Look, Inspector – a large number of trophies have been uncovered by Flopsy's burrowing. I think we've nearly solved the case.	*Clattering of metal.*

	Inspector:	Not quite, Whitsun. We still have to find out who hid them here, and why. Whitsun, we're going to track down the burglars – you'll have to grit your teeth.
Gravel noise. *Footsteps.*	Narrator:	Whitsun duly picked up a handful of sand and began rubbing it into his mouth as they made their way back to the club house and up to the bar.
	Inspector:	Look – there's the bar lady. Beatrix, I'd like a glass of coke and a bag of crisps for my assistant.
Glasses clunk, crisp bag *rustles.*	Beatrix:	Hmmm ... it's not much of a swap but, alright then, here's the coke and crisps.
	Inspector:	Tell me, what have you got in the way of peanuts.
	Beatrix:	Nothing sir. Here they are, look – in full view.
	Inspector:	We're on the trail of some fiendish burglars. We have urgent news – call me the Manager.
	Beatrix:	Alight sir. You're the Manager.
	Mashee:	What's all this then?
	Narrator:	The inspector ignored the Manager's greeting as he peered down his nose.
	Inspector:	Did you know that your nasal hairs are in dire need of a clipping?
Nose blows.	Narrator:	The Manager blew his nose in embarrassment.
	Mashee:	Do you know who the villains are?
	Whitsun:	Yes sir – they're the ones we're trying to catch. We do have one lead.
	Inspector:	Yes – Whitsun picked it up cheap in a pet shop at the railway station.
Clattering of metal.	Mashee:	Give us the trophies then, and you can clear orf. No point in hunting for burglars if we've got the gear back, eh?
	Inspector:	Not so. A crime has been committed and the felon must be brought to trial. Mr. Niblick, I hereby arrest you on suspicion of theft.
	Mashee:	What! This is outrageous. Why do you think it's me?
Huge crash, dogs bark, *loud bleating.*	Narrator:	Suddenly, there was an almighty crash, accompanied by the barking of several loud dogs and the anxious bleating of a confused and lonely sheep. Fortunately for the Inspector, they were irrelevant and only occurred in order to give a bored sound effects engineer something to do.
	Whitsun:	A brilliant deduction, Inspector. How did you guess it was him?

Inspector: Simple. You remember the small lemon-yellow coloured plastic golf ball stand that we found hidden in the bunker, with the trophies? Well, it matches the ones that fell out of Mr. Niblick's pocket when he took out his handkerchief to blow his nose. That particular brand is made specially for the Niblick family.

Whitsun: Brilliant, Guv – how did you do it?

Inspector: <u>A lemon tee</u>, my dear Whitsun. Let's take these villains away and we can get on with our next case. We've got to look for a tall, handsome man for an assault on a large number of voluptuous young women.

Whitsun: Hmmm ... sounds interesting – what's the salary?

The End

Throwing in the Towel

THE CAST
Narrator – a narrator
Inspector Thinkalott – a clever detective
Whitsun – his bumbling assistant
Mollie Coddle – a chalet maid
Herman Von Krautsour – the kiddies' favourite
Grace Kiyes – manageress of the LeisureParx complex

Splashing sound in background.

Narrator:	It was a dark and gloomy night. Probably. Then again, it might have been a bright sunny day. Thinkalott and his bumbling assistant, Whitsun, were enjoying a well-earned holiday and had booked a fortnight's rest at the amazing new indoor LeisureParx complex, where they could enjoy the artificial sunshine to their hearts' content. Under the tinted glass dome, they were oblivious to the real weather, to sunlight, darkness and being caught up in an episode of Changing Rooms. After an early disagreement with the centre's manager, following their attempts at clay pigeon shooting which resulted in some unwanted air conditioning to the centre, they had settled by the swimming pool.
Whitsun:	Isn't it lovely to get away from the hustle and bustle of the police station, to relax here by this lovely pool. Do you fancy a dip?
Inspector:	No thanks, Whitsun. Guacamole always reminds me of a rather nasty cold I once had..
Whitsun:	I mean, let's have a swim – it's one of the best ways to get slim and keep in trim.
Inspector:	I don't believe you... I mean, just look at a whale. Anyway, I'm feeling peckish, it's time we got ready for dinner.

Footsteps.
Vacuum cleaner, blowing sound.

Narrator:	They gathered their belongings and headed for the chalet, where they met Mollie Coddle, the chalet maid, who was busy vacuuming the carpet and puffing up the pillows.
Whitsun:	Excuse me, Mollie, but why are you blowing into those pillows?
Mollie:	Ooh, you are a wag, sir. You seem to spread happiness wherever you go.
Inspector:	He actually spreads happiness WHENever he goes. Anyway, I'm going to take a shower.
Whitsun:	Better leave that to the villains, guv. Police shouldn't take things, remember?
Mollie:	Ha ha ha ha ha ha ha ha....Ha.

40

Inspector:	Enough of that, Whitsun. I'm going to have a bath. Mollie, will you be a dear...?	
Mollie:	Not really, but I can do a pretty neat sheep, and my goat impression ain't bad neither.	*Bleating in background.*
Inspector:	Be gone woman. Whitsun, turn the shower on, will you?	*Water running.*
Whitsun:	How? Do I show it a saucy plumbing catalogue?	
Narrator:	Inspector Thinkalott finally managed to get into the shower cubicle, which was actually a bath standing on its end just in order for the holiday brochure to be accurate when it claimed 'bath AND shower en suite'. It was as he was about to dry himself that he realised something was missing.	
Inspector:	Aaargh! It's gone, Whitsun! It's completely disappeared!	
Whitsun:	Shall I call you a doctor?	
Inspector:	There's no point, Whitsun – I'm a police inspector, not a doctor. Listen, there's nothing wrong with me... it's the towels, they've all been swiped.	
Whitsun:	Have you checked?	
Inspector:	Nope, just plain white ones. Quick, run outside and find me a towel.	*Footsteps, running.*
Narrator:	Whitsun searched in vain for several hours before returning empty handed to the chalet.	
Whitsun:	It's no use, guv. There isn't a towel to be seen. Someone's been pinching them all, according to the centre's Chief Towel Supervisor, Ivor Flannel. All the staff seem to be very upset about the idea of a criminal at loose in the complex.	
Inspector:	Oh dear. Tell me – how's the chalet maid?	
Whitsun:	I believe that they get a few slabs of concrete and bolt them together over precast foundation blocks, but I don't believe that's important right now. Do you think we should get on the case?	
Inspector:	Only if we can't close it in the normal fashion, Whitsun.	
Narrator:	The two officers prepared to scour the complex but quickly realised that they had forgotten to bring enough soap-filled wire pads with them. They decided instead to turn their attention to searching for the mysterious towel-napper. As they trotted around the complex, they soon bumped into Uncle Herman Von Krautsour, 'The Kiddies' Favourite' and part-time comedian, entertainer, charity worker and all-round good bloke.	*Footsteps.*

Herman:	Get out of my way you ugly, pustulant pile of elephant's droppings.
Inspector:	Ah! You must be Uncle Herman, the kiddies' favourite, part-time...
Herman:	Yes, yes... it's me. Now, clear off and play with an electricity pylon won't you? Can't you see I'm busy.
Whitsun:	Sorry sir, but we're on the trail of a mysterious towel-napper. Tell me, have you seen anybody acting strangely?
Herman:	Well, that tall one in Eastenders is pretty rubbish.
Inspector:	Never mind, Whitsun, we've got work to do. First, we must consult the LeisureParx manageress, Miss Kiyes.

Footsteps on gravel. Sneezing, coughing, whistling, birds chirping, trees rustle, sheep bleating, cows mooing, wildebeest grunting, explosion, surprised chickens and turkeys... sound of engineer collapsing!

Narrator:	So saying, they trotted off up the gravel path, conveniently situated in order to give the sound effects engineer something to do. On and on they trotted, sneezing, coughing and whistling merrily as they went, accompanied by the merry chirping of the birds in the rustling trees, the noisy grazing of the nearby sheep, cows and wildebeest and the distant sound of an old power station being demolished with high explosives and falling on an extremely large flock of turkeys and chickens. It was then that the sounds effects engineer collapsed with exhaustion.
Inspector:	We're here.
Whitsun:	So we are, guv. Another brilliant deduction.
Grace:	Hello boys.
Whitsun:	Grace Kiyes, I presume?
Grace:	Who can tell, with the tinted glass dome up there? Anyway, what can I do for you?
Whitsun:	Well, I've been having a bit of trouble with a jigsaw back at the chalet...
Inspector:	We've come about some towel thieving.
Grace:	No thank you – we've already got someone doing that.
Inspector:	I mean that we are the police, or rather, SOME of the police... two of the police to be precise... and I have a plan to entrap the towel-napper for good.
Grace:	Tell me more.
Inspector:	All we need is two large towels and someone who can drive a needle and thread.
Grace:	Look no further. I have two such towels which I was keeping for a rainy day. As for needlework, I am a skilled seamstress – a skill I learnt a few years ago when I was in Iceland.

42

Whitsun:	Iceland, eh? Lovely place.
Grace:	Yes... the thing was, I only went in there for a packet of frozen fishfingers.
Narrator:	The inspector's plan was as simple as Whitsun himself. He and Whitsun lay on one towel, whilst the other was placed on top of them. Grace then sewed the two towels together, cleverly concealing the detectives. She then hung the flannelette version of the Trojan Horse over a specially-reinforced towel rail and waited.
Inspector:	I can hear footsteps, Whitsun. I think we're being pinched by the rotters.
Whitsun:	Ooh-er! I think that we are indeed being manhandled into a waiting car, Inspector.
Inspector:	Lower your voice, you fool.
Whitsun:	But this is as deep as I can speak wearing these trousers. Listen, the car appears to be stopping.
Inspector:	You're right. And now we seem to be being placed upon a table. Quick, let's burst out of here and surprise the crook.
Narrator:	It wasn't until early the next day that they actually managed to burst their way out, due to the skills of Grace and her reinforced thread, but mainly since they actually nodded off for a few hours in the cosiness of their fluffy surroundings. However, when they did emerge, they were greeted by the sight of a large man stuffing towels into cardboard boxes.
Inspector:	Uncle Herman Von Krautsour, kiddies favourite and infamous towel-napper, you are under arrest. We're going to drive you away from here and lock you up.
Herman:	What's the charge?
Whitsun:	It's when a large herd of animals all run the same way, but that's not important right now.
Inspector:	I do believe that you have been stealing each and every towel from this holiday complex and that you have been packaging them up and sending them abroad. What's more, do you know what you call an attraction with big wheels, dodgems and candy floss stalls?
Herman:	It's a fair, cop.
Inspector:	Correct. Tell me, where were you sending all the towels you so cunningly purloined?
Herman:	Ach... I may as vell tell you. I vos sending them to my chums in Spain where ve are undertaking a plan to achieve world domination of sun-loungers. If ve steal enough

Footsteps.

Car stops. Door opens.

Ripping of cloth.

43

towels, we shall soon have enough to place on every sun lounger in ze world!

Whitsun: What a despicable idea.

Herman: I know, but it's ze best that the scriptwriters could come up with.

Inspector: Let's take him to the station, Whitsun.

Whitsun: No need, guv. We've got the car. But you're right, we've got to get him banged up and then we'll have to get back to work.

Inspector: Yes, it's time we sorted out that bloke who's refusing to pay for the double glazing he had installed 12 months ago, on the grounds that the salesman told him it would pay for itself in a year.

Whitsun: Then there's that personal injury case, boss. The one about the butcher who sat on his bacon slicer – what's the latest there?

Inspector: It seems that he's got a little behind with his orders.

The End